moon moon

july westhale

I0139189

moon moon

july westhale

black lawrence press

Black
Lawrence
Press

www.blacklawrence.com

Executive Editor: Diane Goettel
Cover & Book Design: Zoe Norvell
Cover Artwork: "The Dark Side of the Moon" by Slavomir Zombek

Copyright ©July Westhale 2025
ISBN: 978-1-62557-159-5

All rights reserved. Except for brief quotations in critical articles or reviews,
no part of this book may be reproduced in any manner without prior
written permission from the publisher: editors@blacklawrencepress.com

Published 2025 by Black Lawrence Press.
Printed in the United States.

TABLE OF CONTENTS

III.

for Natalie
(& other brightness-dwellers)

the moon's moon must be colder than the moon

and soon we began to rhapsodize about our burning blue
home—

There is no act of forgiveness
higher than metaphor
a body searching
for an exit strategy.

Where we'd once exalted gods
we now pray to canines:
praise to the dog-ears,
the coffee rings, the dented
spines.

The lines hushed
to splayed-apart lips:
roses on walks

in urban landscapes—oh cities! Oh, even garbage
we missed. Garbage could be thrown away.

[we know not what we do]

We know not what we do
except in retrospect,

carved in listless stars,
which cannot dim nor extinguish,
and thank heavens for it—

Without, we'd be lost.
Worse, we'd misunderstand.

I.

like all epics, our heroes begin by suckling genre's breast

If this were prose, it would start
on Sunday, the roundest date
in a week of plump emperors
at a feast of seven fishes:

> days?
> or maybe poems? or teeth?
> like pills on the edge...
> something sonic.
> Possibly glass.

A circuitous way
for a story straight as a bone:
something is like something is like something one step further,
but nothing about Sunday
or heroes, or even breasts,
> and this is why this isn't a novel.

In a poem, Sunday is the teeth of the week.
Did you think the teeth forgotten? Here they are.
Inelegant elegies, that caged the tongue
> that licked the page, turned it, forgot the plot.

in which we landed on the first moon, *in which* the first moon is the womb

Just watch the water, then come
and get me, should it get too full.

    The child watches like a child watching a child.

Rise now, from the dead,
or almost, toys. Bobbing
plastic planets—

    The moon had once been
    ocean, all dried fish to red ash. Soon the moon would

call tide in for supper.
The moon rose from sleep
but the water did not heed. The moon did

    close her eyes again, back to bed.

Concerned the tide
would miss a meal, the child
misunderstands gravitational pull.

    The floor full
    of tide, all orbits at attention.

Sleeping alongside the moon,

a celestial stupor, the eyelids of

death. I AM THE MOON. Water
surrounds her, rises to meet her voice, and outpouring of

stars. Beached, now, the mother taking her

blue silver time. *Here I am, here I am.*
Sorry, sorry. Tide turning

on its side, before falling back to sleep.

the world as it is

When the heroes learned
they could own pieces of the world
they got out their bank cards
and shot the moon. They shorted
the stock of everything optionless,
everything promised: sustained gains!
With overuse, only diminishing returns.

To contextualize: heroes are not angels,
nor demons, nor oracles of the moons
(nor the moon's moon), nor
anthropomorphic. They are, however,
simple. Subway-riding. A spectrum of ordinary.
Maybe you gave one the bird
this morning, on the bridge. Maybe
you are one yourself.

To show it: the world as it is—
a canonized painting, in oils
no one makes anymore. Yet, yet!
Something an artist, with divine
providence, dipped a brush
in a drum of turpentine, and signed.

the world as it is

there's snow on the ocean, which is meant to confuse us
and does, though not because we are unprepared for it
but rather because the sight of it reminds us
of the static-hearted parts of our bodies as we prostrate
ourselves in years-over-yonder: exploratory attempts
to find warmth—not unlike a surefooted expedition—,
in the disappearance of everything ripe—now covered
with snow's annihilating speeches—, in the blank stares
of our children as they amputate themselves from the world,
in the cloudscape of come forgotten to be enjoyed,
on the snow of a down comforter at which we'd first begun
(circle back to exhibit A), in the cold expanse following
the question *am I like winter to you*, in the unspooling
that happens when we, I, I mean I play a memory
over again for the too-many-ith time, in the television's
convex and prudish eye, in the snowy sound of over-use,
in the way empty feels like brain-freeze, in the brilliant
and nearly-neon white of the sign which mourns *vacancy*
even if everyone around us says *off-season*, says they love
the snow, the way it makes well-conquered land possible again.

hero physiology

Mistakes are honest in hindsight.
Love would, of course, continue.
It is the endearing tooth that fails
to catch the loved lips, and the anachronism.
Like this, it changes texture
and look, more failure, this time to hold
love in more accommodating
parts of the body. Say, earlobes
(center of the earth) or behind the knee (moon).
Perhaps freckles (astrology, yes).
Failing these, more failure: to recognize
love's cartilaginous capacities.

Fear not. There is reason, and reason
says *geometry*, says *logic*, says *religious upbringing*.

What's a sense of ethic without a sense
of corporeality? Semantics—
call them failures or pioneers for holding dear
the smell of scalp, a birthmark plumed so like
the shape of a tongue, it tastes the world as it enters it.

the world as volta

      —one day the rain picked up
and left, in a glowing and clear
lack of acoustics.

          It really wasn't
like anyone noticed, except a presence
of an absence. What once was
boisterous and inconvenient
shifted suddenly stifling,
reflective. A formula
with x missing. Nothing to solve for.

public service announcement

people fell ill as they grew sick
as they fought death as they battled bugs
as they zoomed to the finish line
as they stopped to smell gone roses
as they bit the dust as they croaked their thanks
as they turned their hands
into steeples of people
as they stared from windows
lifelining the words, *I should have*
stared from more windows
as the air they made their own-
as the air of their children-
turned against them
as death stopped—

public service announcement

—as they say: fear not
it was kind and gentle and good

this is not a test

let it be said that the animals noticed first

though they are not heroes (see above) (nor
demons, angels, gods, or oracles of the moon's
moon). Equipped with mewlings and lowings
and etymology out of the register
of the heroes' hearing. There was no one
but one another to point to, to yowl
and scratch and stomp and whinny.

Alt: to vowel and consonant and plosive.

When the orders from on high came,
the horses were awake in their human
blankets, their portal eyes covered
in, foreshadow, the fabric of astronauts.

The gods have divined it, but a bit
was placed, cold and silencing,
over the horses' truthful tongues.
So, it came to the cows, the most frequent victims
of the heroes singing. One heifer struck
a lantern with her foot—Chicago,
she thought. Heroes are always blaming
the cows.

> And when the fire vanquished
> the barn and the heroes left their animals
> but took their kin, it seemed clear:
>
> *the gods have divined it, now go.*

six crows hold sermon on a frayed telephone line

and like the mind, which follows a caw
to another and another
the reformed grease birds repent
repent, wash, lather, repent
with their beaks to their wingpits
their mouths open so fully
in picking grit, picking choices (yesterday's
parking lot fries, an acoustic woman's gift flowers)
and, without thought/only prayer, swallowing—

do gods talk to crows

from the mouth of the gift horse:

[I *swear* I was once a colt, eyes to the mirrored
sky, fields of me with ropish legs, coming in
to the feed, the joyful feed, running like bulls
at a festival. The only hands on my flank,
tall grasses that played paramour, played lead,
no weight on my back but the world, which bowed
my body, both the arch of my spine and the curtain
call. Then the call came, which I heard because I am
god. The call and the trucks, the death mask so flies
could not eat my eyes, my brothers gone, no chance
to wave *farewell, farewell* and I *swear* the sky heaved
a pent-up sob. The rumble took me, I sweat and sweat
in my clothes, which smelled of mustangs, other gifts,
and when we at last chanced upon new land, a man
took my hood, and the poet opened my mouth
and shot me gone]

how it is said the world began: big bang

dear children, I know it is difficult to believe in singularity in
an age like ours but consider for a moment that the world was
a bright and barren space at one time—yes, also a challenge to
conceptualize, please keep still, I am telling you a story—and an
incident occurred that lead to another and another and another,
over many billions of—well, no, they don't know exactly the
incident except that it was singular, and yes it is because despite
everything we know we know very little about the Earth's birth,
of course I remember yours, you were early, it was Christmas, I'd
just put dinner in the oven and—they said you were the most
beautiful baby to ever ruin a honey baked ham, but that isn't quite
the same, no, really it's all very complicated because it relies mostly
on math and something called an 'echo', but not like that, please
keep your voice down, there are others trying to sleep—what was
I saying? Yes, an echo, thank you, an echo isn't like hearing your
voice come back to you bigger and stranger but more like tracing
the expansion of the singular incident I told you about, *no, I don't
know* exactly, no one does but you have to have faith in scientists
and astronomers, and what? Well, you're not wrong, faith is
typically a key ingredient in—

how it is said the world began: creationism

once again, nothing: a pure dark
like black slicks before there was color
or slickness but there was, however,
work ethic. Because first there was nothing
(before the nothing was a long line
of ancestral nothings, nothing descending
from seminal nothings like a void orchard)
and then there was everything but something
in there, about light. And seven days, and
Sunday. And rest, which was nihility
before it became an art, an act of closing
these new luminaries called 'eyes'
to remember what nothing felt like.

how it is said the world began: evolution

tree: leaf :: family: _____

_____: species :: tadpole: frog

fate: scattering :: sowing: hubris

faith: heroes :: faulty lifeboat: _____

beginning: end :: end: beginning

for times they think they hang the moon

Are the heroes not like teacups?
Thin lips gilded gold, wide-berthed,
weary of half-mast men and broken
saucers. The marriage bed of pins
and needles adrift in feathers, decked in tulle,
pinned and silken. Take no pleasure
(nor afternoon delight, nor high tea),
or casual stain, however brave the lip.

Shameful, shameful, the rim of the cup,
a sweet, salacious thought, then wiped clean.
Who among us does not love the moon?

(   ).

then the gods said *go,* in the form of vast fires

Fire season is federally
grateful for rain, with municipality
like afterbirth (called *slick*
because a word exists to describe it)
from the belly of something
like the sky, an eternal inconsolable
roaring, a roaring that tastes
like given-up land, which had given up
before the heroes did.

Fires became evidence that the land and sea
spent time between metaphors, that seasons
waited for luminaries to do terrible things
with their celestial bodies. Mostly

it was not the point. Numerology was.
How numerous the burnings, more so
than Horatio's philosophies, Sappho's lovers.
The numerous fires ate all other seasons,
a long and acrid swallow—they ate
everything they loved, then they hate-ate,
including the dead seas, including the once-snow.

with nowhere left to go, the heroes shot for the moon

what you have heard is true—
something rotten once got us
from our houses, from our beds
what was there may
or may not have been.

Remember, my darling, my sweet,
that a blistered and blackened
thing, a thing representing life/
sin itself, was a cause for art.
A lineage. A pride.

The moon rose tonight as usual,
no spore-filled scab. As ivory
as the cut belly of an apple
sliced to share. Nothing noxious
to point to, say *you*.

The world of museums and love
through the machinations
and designations of man-made things,
defined by abstractions: security,
beauty, even, our worst days.

One day, as goes in any epic, a hero or god told his son *yes*.

One day we went balls to the wall for the moon,

we called ourselves both father and son, holy
ghost, too, Odysseus—

the naysayers were in two camps: camp one

when did our nation slip
        the slip under the see-through dress,
        slip between racks of clothes, as a child
        or a child's monster
into this epoch? The post fact
        torture, sophistry, online dating
that we swipe and swipe and use
        oxygen, or chlorine
to clean blood from the roadside. A poet simply can't just
    see a fox as roadkill, and butterflies—
        they must make everything worse. Dance
in intestines with the dead,
    who mean nothing
        until they're dead, especially poets
    with their meaning.

-

(insert quick journey to the underworld, insert a woman who
never wanted us to rescue her in the first place, insert causing chaos
in Hades only to be spit out again, empty-handed, with some
bizarro new skill that is secretly a curse)

-

Everywhere we drive

the dead line the road
like souvenirs.

What's more ideal than afterthought?
(all of the concept behind *throwing shade*)

Roadkill itself is perfect:
no, listen, it is
through the rearview mirror,
a hunched, dead thing
whose guts you will never be
responsible for, something for which you can invent
a better ending, when it occurs to you.

Don't look at us like that.
Don't pretend this poem is about something other than it is.

and what if there are no books on the moon, are the
books' feelings hurt? We want to know if we can smell
the moon, and if it smells like the library of Babel?
And what does truthlook like at the hands of gravity,
and if all our systems are subject
to the principles of floatation, then what
does that say about presence?
What does that say about us? The us-ness of us?

the gods are generous in this way

A moon suit for the Earth! An Earth skin
for the sun! A sunburn for the ice! A taste
of cream on the end of the tongue
when the tongue is tasting skin!

An obliteration of memory in the face
of snow, a blotting out, as if someone
who cared abundantly reached with a hanky
and, like mercy, covered a broken mouth.
Which would be the sea. Too salty
for anyone's taste, anyway, more acid
by day. By night, unearthed creatures
with big fluorescent eyes and too much brain-
power. *Let's blame someone!* the heroes say.
Someone is trashing the Mariana Trench
like their parents are out of town, and this is a movie.

Where were the gods when we needed?
A bacchanal of Earth's closing ceremony,
and only California is dressed properly.
The gods were clocking out, heading to night
life on Mars, or a more-promising Jupiter,
devastating in the off-season,
or the moon's moon. In a show of chivalry,
one last natural disaster, one last tsunami,
a finale of wet so we might say
we saw it! The crowning that could be called *glory*!

as it overtook us, a dress-train of foam and froth
as startlingly cold as we'd ever felt, as abundant
and generous as the world itself, at birth.

[let us be done with this world]

Let us be done with this world, cried the men the men, and take
it upon ourselves to go to the moon, having cast aside this big blue
chance. And up they went to the moon, but it was full, having
short-circuited with *unprecedented* quickness, and so they went to
the moon's moon but found it too brimming with creatures who
refused to be vanquished—

                           meaning, the moons themselves

II.

on the spaceship, which seated only twenty, a man tells
his daughter that the ice below is a fjord

We are not what we are formed by.

The land underneath the plane
is anthropomorphized, a pock mark,
welted, marking the moment
of impact, of violent change.
It's a very human error,
grafting. It makes smaller
pieces matter only as a big picture
whole. Like an archipelago.
I am not only not what I am formed by
but often I am failed by etymology.

The father does not tell the child this.

on watching a woman watching a man tell a story of
the world to a listening child

At first, he did not notice the gentle hum of bees as they
left but then, like everyone, he forgot them altogether.
This is either the structure that does not allow men to
proverbially ask for directions or an inability to notice cold
chaos—or, terribly, both.

hero philosophy 101

one would never guess it (oh, good, a game!),
but here we are many days without our bouncing
blue ball, our terrestrial ball and chain, our baby
planet—not even a note as it slipped from the rearview.
Now a footnote in a book that, were we on said earth,
a man would walk door to door to sell as a collection:
The History of Aquamarine, Abridged.

                    But we are not earthlings
any longer, with no taxonomical replacement in sight. O, stars
coronate the endless black, winging it,
                              and here we are:
                              the most select tourist.
The most inclined to shoot
the earth for the moon's moon, to go nil,
to bankrupt because it is the most American thing to do.
Reminder to self: nationality was left behind
with the linens, currency, non-heroes.
No matter nationality—
only the home, the journey to and from.

Reminder to self: let us not
       seek solace from the callousness of quietude, for it is what exiled
       us.

enter the oracles and other Others

at the entrance to the moon's moon, which was merely a half day's
     journey
from the moon proper, stood two oracles, shifting towards and
     about-face
in proximity to one another. Think of all the fantastical elements
of space aesthetic: they had them. Think two Whitneys: Preacher's
     Wife,
and Israel. You want them to wear white? They do. And if you like
your auguries technicolor, that can be arranged. What was
     inarguable
was that they turned to the open-mouthed citizens of the ship's
     interior,
muttered something that sounds like *enter—*

log from unknown hero, date rubbed off

*fine morning (hard to tell): wind strong enough to blow many
untethered possessions from their posts, temporary as they are. Dull
prospect for making contact with any form of life though the stars
seem to grow ever more plentiful the more I look at them. Landscape
is like a dry dusty sponge. It suits those from the American southwest,
but the southerners are already attempting to fashion humidifiers.
There is nothing to lead us to believe this is hostile land and yet there
is nothing else, either*

It was too dark and then we were alone

it was terrible   right?   yes.   it was

enough to convince a body to transubstantiate
or to become like terror itself: a terror loaf.

no.   it wasn't.   that's not quite   truth, nor approaching

a gospel remotely adequate. do I mean
dread? also associated with weight, weighty. and terrible.

in epics   in voltas   the world becomes

the underworld redeems. heroes die or don't die, and not
for being alone—that they strive for. solitude: a mantel.

yes   it was lonesome.   is that better   perhaps

why didn't someone find me
was there even something to look for

when we reached the moon's moon, we were surprised it had two capital cities, like Bolivia

It was like stepping into a basin of lights, a bowl of half-dimmed
stars, to the urban dwellers among
    us. For the bucolically inclined, it was *too much*. But that's
    the thing

we enjoyed about it. Enjoy. Present tense. Still enjoyable in the
glass elevator of one's memory, even
        if there is a child at the helm, pushing all the buttons. You
        cannot

go up and down at the same time, but you can be surrounded by
something that is so potently
        unique that it has its own year, takes its own time reaching
        your eyes. By that

I mean light. I mean a country with two capital cities. I mean the
way you hold grapefruit—it knocks
        me out. However, it didn't hurt. Not only because we are
        far from home. I mean, new home.

But because I'm sorta invincible. In other countries, and space, too,
it turns out. The other country
        of a banging heart, or some place in my insides that feels
        knock-kneed.

The hollow bereavement of a city in blackout, say, or the turned-
inside-out shake of standing after

    falling. Something continued to fall, straight to the earth,
      which is all light

molten and crushed-up, as though the inverse of La Paz is a mortar
and pestle. Electricity an

    afterthought. Who am I kidding. We all feel this way.

did we pass heaven

or was it another ball of gas? And did something wave
in a way that meant waving, but looked to us like nothing?
Were there other creatures, and did they understand us?
Does it matter to us more to be understood, or to inhabit?
Do we have to choose?

Those of us who would survive the trip to the moon,
then to the moon of the moon, would question
whether we'd seen any Others or oracles at all—
not that we ever talked again, that we ever admitted
how foolish we were, to believe
the gods would divinely guide us, then to believe again
that a cow would be the angel, David.

But the Others—they visited when everyone was sleeping.
They had no shape, but were luminaries as luminous
as wattage itself. As close as any of us could have come
to traveling near heaven in a fiberglass ship. One glance
into the triptych of how our world, and all others, began
and ended, much more numerous and complex
than language, our stories as insufficient
as our earthly bodies, our terrestrial limitations—
even as we became inhabitants of space, as we called
ourselves moon gods—

in which the heroes become the antagonists

The heroes, as predicted, began to think of themselves as
   gods.
The heroes had no one to challenge them.
The heroes set about turning the dry lunar landscape into
   topographical fantasy.
They built raised beds without plants to bury, they built
   libraries without books to read.
They built the brightest side of the moon's moon into a
   grand cathedral, without divinities
to worship. It was then that they began to worship
   themselves. It was then that alters were
erected, and confessionals whose only allowable confession
   was disbelief in the hero-gods.
The hero-gods began to return to a state that was pre-
   creationism; the nothing spread between them like a
   darkening flood. Individualism was lost. Singularity
   was lost. It seemed to them that they had everything
   they ever needed. They tried for fire…

capital city number one

Q: how is the bright side of the moon's moon like a
confessional?
A: I came to talk sins

Q: do your sins have placement here? Do you disbelieve?
A: I confess I cannot stand the eternal burning of the stars
around me, the specters of luminaries at night, the lack of
light but totality of a soft glow—everything is neither dark
nor light. I confess I want more to confess to—my breath
to close the gap between air and not air, to remember the
prayers I learned as an earthling child—

Q: what is prayer in space?
A: I thought you knew?

Q: what is prayer in space?
A: a sonic boom of *fuck fuck fuck*

Q: what are the hero gods like in space?
A: exactly the same

> A: no room at the inn for the girl, and
> the world, and the sky, and the moon.

aubade for earth

morning has broken   like the first morning
moon gods are singing *like the first* creatures

what distinguishes an aubade from a nocturne
is night and day—lovers are lovers
if they can leave.

In the black sea of space, our tourmaline
beloved dogpaddles, taken for granted.

Even the most brilliant side of the moon
is not morning—birds are birds
because of morning. It is not

so much a hymn to the earth abandoned
as it is to the container that contained.

nocturne for earth

the darkest side of the moon's moon
is nearly the relief
of a nightmare

o cosmonaut, o astronaut, o all-for-naught

We got lost but instead of being frightened
we grew bored. We grew bored so tall
notches on the doorframe outgrew
the house, then the block, then the entire
municipal grid, and the greenbelt surrounding it.
Two paths in a wood (but only one head
for sense). Many lips, however (too many lips).

Did we say *sense?* We meant the nose. We meant
the factory of olfactory, the senses
like locomotives, the motives lost, but then so lost
they got bored and left us. Where were we? Ah,
yes, static—one small step for man, one giant
one for sensibility.

> There are plans and secret plans and
> then there's the startling (small start!)
> epiphany.

capital city number two

Remind me why we journeyed forward to begin with, o home(r),
o Gilgamesh, o cosmonaut, o astronaut, o all-for-naught? And
when we fumble the dust holds our struggle just or maybe un-
like sand on Earth where water makes clear we weren't there.
But no tides scour the empty seas, pocking. Instead, our raw soles
canter along, impressions left—narrative of a place
more place than place itself.

> Raw, but here. How
> unfashioned, this moon!

**the day the rescue ship came from our old blue base, you were in
the moon's moon's ocean**

alone, which is against everything Californian public education
teaches: do not swim alone, do not turn your back—

did you even know there were oceans on the moon?
There aren't. But there are great divots of space, of speculation

maybe water was once here, maybe it filled a hole

because there are no fish nor sand dollars nor takeout bags
nor grasping fingers of kelp

there is no choice but to be alone, alone as in the womb,
alone as wombhood, which is to say, the very

aloneness of alone, the sky and dust and great expanse of lack
orbiting *lonely alone lonesome*

> interrupted by an intercom, the
> foreign public-school crackle
> of sound amplified: *we have come for
> you, help has landed, we will take you home*

III.

it is too easy to say mirage

The oracles never said *enter.*
The oracles had no mouths, no tongues.
The oracles were not oracles at all.
The oracles were trick images of temperature, like those in Phoenix.

When scientists and astronomers traveled back to the moon's moon
many years later to research and explore this ill-begotten settlement,
they found no guardians to the entrance, no indication of an
entrance at all. No trace of the church, libraries, or other buildings
the heroes, as they called themselves, built seemed to remain. Only
a few circles surrounded by structures that seemed like benches:
like fire pits for cooking, for warmth. Upon further inspection, no
evidence of ash or char or flame.

are there ghosts on the moon's moon

and if so, which side
and if so, what can we learn
from the traceless prints
their bodies made, the indelible
mark they left, in the lonely, lonely dark?

[as the scientists headed back to their ship]

As the scientists headed back to their ship, one cried out—*here!* At the brightest side of the moon, where the settlement was said to have landed, were soft outlines in the dust, imprints of bodies in motion: moon angels, facing one another.

genesis

It is simple, really. At the beginning of the world there was one earth, and the earth expanded. It *echoed* out from an unknown, gate-kept singularity. It was after nothing, but before the days of the week. The earth came from another species of earth, which beget many more versions of itself. The earth expanded so far that it combusted and the inhabitants, who'd sought expansion in the first place, said *too far!* too late. The earth died one hundred thousand times. The earth was shorted, but the earth is the one thing that should never be shorted. Never shoot the moon on the earth. Never shoot the moon on the moon. On the moon's moon, one has a chance of shooting, but there's only oneself to shoot.

Acknowledgments

There is an entire moon's moon of people who make a book come into the world. Here is a woefully inaccurate attempt to thank some of mine: Natalie Ponte, Michael Mercurio, Joey Gould, Carl Phillips, Pam Houston, Dana Belott, and Em Bowen. Thank you to Diane Goettel and Black Lawrence Press, for welcoming this weird little book into the family.

With unending gratitude to Writing by Writers and the Tom and Evelyn Newbury Fellowship, Poets & Writers, and the University of Arizona.

Versions or fragments of these poems appeared in *Lily Poetry Review, Prairie Schooner, Hayden's Ferry Review,* and *Calyx*.

Poet and translator **JULY WESTHALE** was born in the American Southwest. Their books include *moon moon, Trailer Trash, Unmade Hearts,* and *Via Negativa,* which Publishers Weekly called "stunning" in a starred review. Ocean Vuong chose Westhale as the 2018 University of Arizona Poetry Center Fellow. Their translation of the Chilean poet Rolando Cardenas' collected works was selected for the 2026 Unsung Masters Series (forthcoming from Pleiades Press). They have work in *McSweeney's, DIAGRAM, The National Poetry Review, Prairie Schooner, CALYX, Hayden's Ferry Review,* and *The Huffington Post,* among others. July is represented by Carolyn Forde at Transatlantic and lives in Tucson, where they are adapting their novel to film. www.julywesthale.co